D0546364

My

Brother

Is Getting

Arrested

Again

PITT POETRY SERIES

Ed Ochester, Editor

My

Brother

Is Getting

Arrested

Again

Daisy
Fried

UNIVERSITY

OF PITTSBURGH

PRESS

The publication of this book
is supported by a grant from
the Pennsylvania Council on
the Arts

Published by the University of Pittsburgh Press,
Pittsburgh, PA 15260

ISBN 0-8229-5919-4

BETTER READ, A VALENTINE

Scare, tides & herring. Shift. Sky
at night. Eye flight, the plane half empty.
Light district, letter days, in tooth

and claw. Hot Chili Peppers, blooded,
lobster, roses, River Valley,
remember? Flag flying here

(though cowards flinch
and traitors sneer). Rover.
Rover, come over.

FOR JIM

CONTENTS

I.

II.

III.

I.

Cordless

I was feeling interesting. I was feeling fragile
so I thought I'd call
and leave you a message.

I was lying around listening to girl singers
on college radio with their guitars singing of pain,
thinking I could do that, though I couldn't,
though they're all so awful with their fake little-girl voices.
Wait, I've got another call, hang on,
no, I'll call you back.

OK, that was a girl, she sounded about 12,
she thanked me for joining Amnesty International,
she talked like this: I'd like to tell you? about how thousands
of people? suffer torture and prison? around the world?
just for speaking out against their governments?
So can you send an emergency contribution?

I was feeling like wax paper, cellophane, ashes.
I said I didn't think she should be asking for more
money when I just joined three weeks ago. She said like
the whisper at the end of an orgasm ohhhhh-kayyy.
Such a sigh.

Did I tell you I can't drink for ten days? I blame you.
You made me go to the doctor. You said "oh, no,
don't go, all that can happen is you can die." The doctor
said it's either Lyme disease or strep. More tests I could
not afford so he gave me this powerful antibiotic
which is supposed to knock out whichever. Drinking
would interfere with the medication. I do blame you.

3

I was feeling like the phlegm in my throat, like I could
dissolve in a cough, and re-form. I was feeling like
heated glass, a rusted edge, a furnace core, I was feeling
burnt black in spots. I was feeling like snot, sweat,
spit and cum going dry on couch fabric, going dark,
then light and dry again, and feathering off.

Hear that buzz? It means I've got this cordless phone
too close to the refrigerator which means I'm too close
to the beers, eleven cold pale beautiful beers. Silos,
horns, test tubes of delight.

I did find a tick on me. It was hooked in my scalp.
I had to pull it down along my hair; pieces
of it squashed off as I pulled. I found it while I was
sitting on the couch, leaning on Ralph, his hair still all
wet from coming in up my walk out of the rain. I
threw it on him. I would have thrown it on you if
I'd been sitting on you, not the dog.

I don't want to go back to the doctor so I better
get better. He took one look at me. He said "what are you,
burning the wick at both ends?" Well, I want to know,
what do people do in the evening when they can't drink?
I don't mean you, you read. Oh somebody get me a
guitar. Or get me a job? With Amnesty International?
So you aren't my boyfriend yet? But I am
addicted to your skin?

I have to go lie down now. I'm not feeling
very brave. I am feeling like
there is nothing left
in the world except me in this house alone.

Doll Ritual

Spanking the bad, kissing the good ones, that's a thrill,
poor things. Mornings I lay out all the teds and dollies
with their bald spots, coy looks, rag bodies, hysterical eyes.
Some with chewed-off noses. Some, patches where snot,
pee, has dried. The one I name Ti-Anne, my favorite, my doll
afraid of all the others, with broken eyelids supposed to flip up
stuck shut? Her I sit to one side to watch the whippings.
Her namesake, Ti-Anne (don't ask), my best enemy (I have
lots of enemies, she's the only one I name a doll for) has eyes
those same types of hysterical colors, changes them daily.
She licks her fingers before she tries to stick them in my eyes.
No one yells but someone sings *ha ha.* "Ti-Anne, Ti-Anne,"
I call, "you stink!" and you know the bad girl smashes my lunchbox
thinking it's my face. I'm thinking about this, I see my pattern:
incitement, paralysis, incitement, paralysis. Why can't you
ever handle what you start, little girl? See, I have never
been poor at all, except just an indigence, also
a mendacity, of heart; and the way I think it's otherwise.

American Brass

The percussionist is the only skinny member
of the American high school marching band
playing the Luxembourg Gardens bandstand
under overspreading horse-chestnut trees.

The massy, meat-bound, milk-fed teens
hold their tubas like dads hold pubescent
daughters. Like they're too big
to be held. Like they love them like babies.

Now the boy trombonist steps forward.
His band jacket hangs open around a heavy
belly he's too young for. He begins a solo
designed to show how slow he can play,

and how fast. Impossible to know why
French people stay for these ineptitudes.
But they do, and we do, Jim and me,
tap our feet and kindly clap. Ah, their children

run around in the dust. They run with sticks.
Lummox clouds push over, abut, stay put,
drop drizzle that hardly manages its way
through the cover of hand-shaped

leaves that touch and touch together. Ah,
the Paris children are running under them
with sticks in chic baby clothes: not pinks,
not blues—oranges, oxbloods, olives.

The man who announces the songs is proud
of his translations. "Et maintenant," he says,

"'Home on the Range.' Ou, (pause) 'Maison sur
l'espace ouvert.'" House on the Open Space!—

gets me and Jim giggling. And I think,
as the boy takes up his trombone again,
the French see in American brass the U.S.A.
they loathe and love: something beautifully crass.

We all love what others have done wrong to.
Last night we went to hear writers of serious
American westerns at an English-language
bookstore—upstairs room, chairs shoved

among shelves, too many books, people,
carpet grubby—stories where Indians and bears
kept wandering and seeking. At the Q&A,
the half-mad bookstore owner kept abusively

asking, "ze bear in your story, he symbols
somezing, no? American violence? ze bombing
of Serbia?" I whispered to Jim, "yeah, well,
what about the French in the '60s in Algeria?"

(I was so pissed.) In the metro that night,
four cops hassled an Arab, machine guns
strapped to their backs. The Arab: resigned,
half-scared. Everyone just kept looking

away, going by. But here I am now, under
these trees with this iffy, distant weather,
thinking about, well . . . swans, wishing
for tragic swans to land their alien selves

under this green bigtop, walk among us,
do a comic dying swan act—real swans

in their feathers, not girls in tutus, and they'll
dance *Swan Lake*—to "Home on the Range."

What if they pecked and plucked the sticks
away from the children, laid their pellet-heads
in the lap of, say, that man there with his dark blue,
red-piped, gold-buttoned blazer and perfect

white hair. Or in the lap of my husband, Jim.
Now trombone boy pulls to a shaky end—
we ought to go but we sit a long time more,
holding hands, listening to American

brass filling up all of every thing, the trees,
the park, these interrupted spaces, paths,
kids, dust, the French, our hearts, with its
sound like money, like bombs falling in air,

bombs falling now on Afghanistan.

May '01 / Jan. '02

Neat Hair

The college kids are all taking their hairdos
out for walks, Indian summering around,
lying this way and that in hip mounds, lotus
positions, jeansie angles. You think college

kids don't have hairdos? That they are
something else—scrub, tatter? Think again:
across the plaza, popular for its coincidence
of hiddenness and, well, popularity,

hair is obvious like choruses of singers
arrayed on risers like beauty shop wigheads
suddenly gone stylish. My sunstruck book
is one more aging poet's particular calibration

of ostentatious deepthink, wist- or rue-
or manfully facing mortal intimations.
Sigh, close book, look up. Certain girls'
paneled shirts and skirts blow in the wind.

The more lovely for their being aware of it.
The wind also is in the trees. The trees are
like Bozo the Clown. The upper branches
bare, sun glaring them into a drab brilliance,

bald as a head. The lower all orange, gaudy,
or a screaming red. The kid who asked me
where's the physics lab goes on his way.
Neat hair. First boy ever to call me ma'am.

Shooting Kinesha

"I hate what I come from," says my cousin Shoshana,
22, jawing per always, feather earrings tangling
in her light brown hair. Shoshana hangs onto Kinesha,
her kid, to stop her running off. Our cousin Deb's
wedding just got out; we're standing at the bottom
of the wedding hall steps. "White people
don't have culture, except what they stole
from our African brothers." Shoshana's
wearing black, per always, me too, her in leather,
me in acetate-velour. "Weddings, U-G-H."
Shoshana spells out *ugh* like it's spelled
in books. "I hope yours was cooler than this."
I nod. I always nod at Shoshana, whatever she says.
Shoshana checks, rechecks her watch, waiting
for her boyfriend. I'm waiting for my husband too.
I've been a pain in the ass to him all morning.
Shoshana sips cheap California champagne
to hide her upset feelings. Kinesha breaks loose,
veers close to the street and parked cars and traffic,
thrashes her lace anklets and buckle shoes
into a crowd of part-white pigeons.

"In London I only hung out with Jamaicans,"
Shoshana says. "People gave me looks on the bus.
Ouch." She detangles an earring. "Once I ripped
an earlobe on these. Anyway, I want you to meet
my boyfriend. He's cool, he's sticking by me.
He says he knew he could when I wouldn't
dime him out after they caught me with his pot
at the Kingston airport. Kinesha's his. He's
the only guy I've loved since, you know, Ken?"
Ken's the one who died beside her

of an overdose in the Motel 6 in Ohio
the time she was 16 and stole her dad's Beamer
to run away. "You heard?" Of course I did,
in this family. "Kinesha's Kinesha
to remember him," she says. "I still miss him."
I nod. I poke Kinesha's belly, her nose.
"U-G-H," says Kinesha, annoyed. I'm bad with kids.
"I'm teaching her to assert herself," Shoshana says.
Her wrist-chains jangle. I twist my wedding ring.
An organ somewhere plays "Ode to Joy."

Here comes the third bad cousin, Christina,
scruff-haired in the pale pink prom dress
her sister the bride made her wear. $90,000
per year doing something with websites and she
can't even keep her hair in order. "Isn't it awful?"
Christina says. "What do I look like, Gwyneth Paltrow?
You guys look swell." She's good with kids:
Kinesha slams herself for a hug into Christina's
legs. Christina and Kinesha kiss. She says
"Did you like my PowerPoint Presentation
on the bride's life? Did you think it was funny?
Go play with the pigeons." She puts Kinesha down.
"Deb wanted a poem, but don't you hate poems?
Was it wrong of me to start with an Eminem quote?"
Kinesha shouts, staggers, stamps at the pigeons;
jaded, they hardly move, only jump-start
half-hearted when Kinesha brandishes
her one-armed naked Barbie above her head,
then turns Barbie into a gun, shoots
at them. "I feel like we should be
sneaking around back with cigarettes
like we used to, remember?" says Christina.
"Too bad we don't smoke anymore."

Shoshana takes out her Newports, lights up.
I'm remembering we never much liked each other,
only hung together at family gatherings
because we were supposed to be the bad ones.
I hate what I come from. I say "My father
just told me again my poems are 'too full
of disgusting sex.' He said 'Why don't you
write more like Derek Walcott?' I'm sick
of him throwing serious deepthinking
genius men up at me." Christina rolls
her eyes, shakes her head, fudges hair tendrils
back into her frizzy twisted updo, vibrates
her lips, blows air out. "Can you tell I'm
drunk already?" she asks. I nod. She shrugs.

Shoshana checks her watch. "I'm gonna kill him."
I wish I wanted to kill my husband.
Right now, I hate everything, everybody,
and don't have a friend in the world
except my husband. It's true he dislikes me
more and more these days but at least
he likes my poems and hates Derek Walcott.
Kinesha sprays Barbie-bullets at everything,
Barbie's head as bald as her elided crotch.
"I didn't buy her that racist, sexist doll,"
says Shoshana. Christina and I nod.
"She found my old one. I pulled
all her hair out when I was 14
and shaved my head the first time."
Kinesha moves away from the settling pigeons,
turns her Barbie gun on us, shoots.
Rat-a-tat-tat. "Ugh, you got me,"
we say, and "BANG!" I say. We turn
our hands into guns, three bad cousins,

Mother, Bridesmaid, and me, Wife-and-Daughter,
for all our different reasons, shooting the child.

Best of Show

I hear the thumps and screams
and run to see a sow gone mad in her pen.
She slams her fat weight at the slats.
They shake, crack. She falls, fed up victim
of feeding up, her meaty body rolling.
She screams, gets up on her trotters,
whangs again. Smell of raw wood.

A crowd gathers, maybe in horror. The boy and girl
hired hands whisper urgent calm. Shouldn't there be a vet
who can stick this thing with tranquilizers? Where's the farmer?
"Playing pinochle back at the truck," the boy says.
"Well go!" the teen girl screams in a whisper,
and smacks his shoulder, and he runs off.

Like a polaroid developing on her Dick Cheney skin,
the pig's capillary patterns emerge purple, thready network
responding to breakage. It was always there, under.

In the arena,
a steer steps out of his nub-furred stillness,
finds that stillness again a step ahead.

The girl helper climbs half up
the pen slats maybe thinking to climb over
and give the sow a hug. The sow
slams her body at the slats the girl stands on.

The sow's hide effloresces
to open abrasions, a whole wallpaper
of bloody begonias. The crowd bristles
relief. A smell antiseptic now, half-straw, half-shit,
something with fear, something like sex.

In the arena the steer pulls an impossible
weight-load on pallets. The crowd applauds.

Seven Years

These cold days when the insane sky's clear, heat poofs away beyond its net of edible blue. My cat folds, flops across the laundry steps. Flags the size of jeans pockets flip-flap affixed to rowhouse fronts. The nicest, cleanest hands reach to switch out lights in stores: futons, ring trays, eyeglasses, dresses, go dark. "The bed is not very big." Cold or no there are fathers calling mothers and children walking home or out; also those of us who are neither father nor mother and have forgotten the complicated unchosen knits and methods of being somebody's child. Hires Root Beer signboard creaking, then not creaking. This year Thanksgiving dinner begins in the afternoon: a moist bird, venison stuffing. Window glass goes blue-indigo. "Is this the right crockery?" Cold little birds, like knots of twine, jam the Japanese Zelkova just outside, gabble in light-loss hysteria. The Dow Jones dropping. Friends' kids leer from photos I stuck on the refrigerator. Last night I slammed a door so hard the mirror hung on it shattered over my back. I was not hurt; moreover he stopped shouting back, ran in his socks onto the crackling glass, put his arms around me?

Jubilate South Philly: City 14

For I will consider how to be 14.

For will you please not act like you know me?

For quit talking to me like I'm a kid.

For when I walk I keep my shoulders crooked back.

For I walk in threes, looking bright into the distance as if I'm more concerned with something else. For if I am one, I am not the prettiest, just the one who holds my shoulders farthest back, hems my uniform skirt the highest, so the space between my kneesocks & skirt is exceeding pure, is good to think on, if a boy would express himself neatly. For I know just how to sneer to get a boy to like me.

For if I am two, my fat, which is beautiful, pushes out in the gap between my shirt & low-rise jeans. I snap my gum, blow bubbles the size of Spalding balls, wear dark eyeliner, line my lips' outer edges with a different dark than my lipstick's pink. For the tattoo I want at the base of my back that my mother won't let me get is a rising sun, the flames of it just licking up out of my jeans.

For if I am three, I am sort of shy & pretty, I sort of go along & wish my parents would let me stay out later & no one notices me, & my friends are so funny, the funniest, the coolest, I wish I could be so funny & cool.

For at the first glance of the glory of Frankie on Seventh St. who has his learner's permit, I worship in my way.

For I wreathe my body seven times around with elegant quickness. For I leap up to catch the musk of his aftershave [though he doesn't really need to shave], which is the blessing of Frankie upon my prayer.

For I roll upon prank to work it in, i.e., sometimes he touches my elbow & I think I'll never wash again.

For last year everyone had henna tattoos & little stretchy chain chokers & this year without saying anything, no one's wearing them anymore, why didn't I notice?

For I look up at my friends for instructions.

For we go in quest for food: jalapeño poppers, Diet Cokes, cheesesteak with.

For I can tread to all the measures upon the musick: Shakira, Eve, Christina Aguilera . . .

For I have this certain gesture: I bend my arm up, crook my hand, fingers somewhere between loose & tense, palm down.

For accompanying the gesture, I let loose a little sharp breath.

For I go tsk!

For I have HAD IT, I'm UP TO HERE!

For OK, it's overdramatic, it's too much, but like what am I supposed to do, spraggle upon waggle at the word of command?

For I shall yell at my sister.

For I am tenacious of my point.

For ohmigod Reenie just went & got her bellybutton pierced & her mother's gonna kill her. No she ain't says Reenie, & everybody giggles so hard they're leaning sideways.

For they are falling down almost.

For at 14 I am not too young to be sexy & not too old to fight with the nine-year-olds on the block.

For *naaaoooooowwwooooo!* I cry, & *fu-uuuck yeeaaooowww* I say.

For the doubling of diphthongs is the improvement of the arguer's talent.

For we stand in the light on the corner again tonight, the boys come around like most times, & this old man, like 35 at least, says you girls get home what are you doing out so late & Reenie sasses him & he walks away & ohmigod it's so funny.

For shall I not be good & sweet?

For shall I not be important?

For I am mean to the dog.

For I swear at it. Then I am nice to the dog, see how nice, see how animal-loving, I hug this furry thing, & bury my face, my only friend. Ew, you smell, get away from me.

For I brush my hair hard; it snaps & floats heavenward.

For in brushing of it I perceive light about it both wax & fire.

For then I apply Frizz-Ease & I bless the name of John Frieda that
my hair is all better.

For shall I buy green or orange sneakers?

For maybe if I am fourteen I am six months pregnant & everybody
looks sad when they see me & I don't know which is the father.
Don't care, & none of them hang with me anymore anyway.

For I don't care because they always stole all my cigarettes anyway.

For I'm quitting, I really am.

For I hope it was Frank. For he called me once since.

For my face is so puffy, but I don't even care. For I don't even know
why.

For nothing's on TV & Ma won't pay for DSL.

For I would never get an abortion, Ma won't let me.

For Ma will take care of it & it will be fun to dress up.

For on the Broad St. Line the other day I heard what they were
saying.

For anyway Shell rode me on the back of her bike & we screamed
cause my belly was pressing into Shelly's back & we were
laughing so hard it was so funny?

For dumb old Shelly said I told you you better stop riding with
those boys, it won't lead nowhere but the bedroom, now see?
At least I had fun while she stayed home.

For I always put dried roses in my bedroom.

For I tell everyone I always put dried roses in my bedroom.

For the goddamn air conditioner is broken.

For even so I can swim for life. For I can creep.

For it is hot out & where do I go, pregnant, on a summer day?

Broken Radios

My neighbor's wife sits in a lawnchair
on the city cement sidewalk, fingers
the dials of several broken radios. Blistery
twisting fingers lose their color, whiten
from grasping. She brings static, blended,
weeee-ooo-ookkkk, down upon us. News
from such satellite singers as pass beyond
the seeable sky. Her eyelash brush has left
its own celestial smudge over one brow.
Handy she was, I heard. Fixed things.
Her car. The sink. Took care of him.
Boxed at the gym even, in middle age,
skipped, bounced, pummeled the bag.
Worked efficiently at a job job. Then,
nothing. Strange early stroke: nothing.
Her husband yanks her knit cap lower
on her head despite summer's heat,
spanks at her pale twiddling fingers.
It seems to me we should all look up
and right about now maybe a cloud should
explode. "It seems to me," my husband says,
"everything he does shows he beats her.
In the house, at night, beats her."
I don't think so.
The really good thing about a husband
is besides his thoughts, his body, turning,
turning, always turning towards you,
there's a whole other part of him
that won't turn or be known, which is
present, past, future, even as the world
constantly unsheathes its averaging
literalness. Out here, we are so naked.
He is much more naked than she is.

Gal Noir

oh Lana Turner we love you get up
    Frank O'Hara, *"Poem"*

Nothing familiar, nothing sugarcoatable, I left
the hospital board of managers reception
a little drunk. Not drunk—on two Camparis
and a lager?—a little warmed and silly-feeling,
saying things I should have known not to say.
It seems the nurses are all fond of discussing
the murders: the greasy river, the bloody wrench,
the dog pound, the grave in the woods,
the beautiful Cuban, Marina, a class act;
the chop shop with its giant car crusher
Toots the towtruck driver calls "My Uncle Vinnie—
takes care of difficult problems," with a pointed
leer. All that segued on my leaving into the ugly
mood of the crowd pressing at the entrance as
the bigs and I went through the automatic door.
Who could blame them? They wanted answers.
Me too. But the drinks made me panicky, sluggish
narcotized panic, I turned up the collar
of the knockoff Burberry raincoat I picked up
for cheap from a guy in a bar on the southside.
I put my nose down into it, pressed my shades
up closer to my face. "You don't think too much,
you just keep going": Dad's words rang in my ears,
and I flashed on my one memory of Ma—her apron
and gravy smell. Nervous, I ran across
under the porte cochere to retrieve my jalopy
from the far end of the parking lot, praying for once
it would give me a break and start. At the back
of the jostling crowd, a familiar nod my way
from one or two I didn't recognize—how you know

you're semi-famous. Or was there something more in it—
something I ought to be worrying about? Above,
pieces of the zodiac would have been wheeling
only I couldn't see them sunk as I was inside the city,
all its bleary polluting light. I should have
been figuring something out—should I call
Jackie, my contact at the United Mine Workers local?—
my sketchy sleep patterns of late were taking
a serious toll on my thought processes. Also
I kept thinking how not two hours since
he and I shared our thoughts till my hands got to
interesting places on his body, places hard and soft,
also my mouth, me worrying all the time that
everything I did really only annoyed him.

The Falling

Wind pulls leaves down off
    the big schoolyard oak by the fence.
        Damp-cold on our faces. We gang
            at the gate, fifth graders. 8:46.
                Ugly Emily runs into the yard,

hands out, *catch the leaves! catch*
    the leaves! shouting in the leaf-swirl.
        Leaves in her hair. Leaves
            in her sweater. Nose plugged as usual
                by snot, teeth sticking out,

can't even close her mouth.
    Oak limbs shaking. *Catch the leaves!*
        Catch them! So we do, fifteen of us,
            running spiky circles, fingers up
                like traps on our arm ends. Boy ties

flap, girl legs smacked by our skirts,
    knees red in the cold. *Look at her, so happy,*
        you think we're going to like you
            tomorrow? Scuzzbag, boogerface,
                snot-mouth, buck-tooth, four-eyes. Still

we're a long time at it this morning,
    catching down leaves, plucking them
        out of their falling high up as we can,
            laying them to ground gentle, same as
                they would have been without us.

II.

Aunt Leah, Aunt Sophie and the Negro Painter

Under the lemon, the goblet, the plate of grapes, painterly,
late cubist, by a WPA artist—"the Negro"—
her sister knew in Chicago, my Aunt Leah sits:

"Your father giving his atheist mother
a religious funeral with that schmuck rabbi—why?"
She taps her cigarette, neat fingernail, puts it down,
points the back of her head at the painting.
"Your Aunt Sophie wanted you to have it."
Her cigarette smokes up a thin blue-gray plume.

Sophie was a Socialist. "Communist," Aunt Leah says,
tilting her recliner. "I was the Socialist. Sophie went
to the Peekskill Robeson concert with the Negro painter."
She blows smoke-ribbons up past her eye. "They got
beat up, mobs, cops, nightsticks. I gave them tea—
they came over after. The painter's head was sticky
with blood." Leah exhales nostril-smoke at her chest.
"I laughed at them. 'What did you expect?' I said."

Last time I saw Sophie she was in bed
at the constant care center, cursing
at OJ, fiddling with the edge
of her bedspread. The room stank
of medicine. The painting hung
gray-blue over the TV.

I hoist up from my chair in Leah's home,
look where the palette knife or artist finger
touched wet canvas. I cock my head
side to side; window sun reflects off
the frame-glass, blots out the fruitbowl.
Leah says,

"It's student work, 1938. Sophie told him
'go out to the street, paint your people.'
So he did. And never got famous.
Communists were wrong about
art and everything else. That's how Stalin
became a monster and messed everything up—"

To stop another lecture on the purges
I tell Leah how my sister promised
to take my cat while I was on honeymoon;
then, day of my wedding, wouldn't. "I don't
remember why. She screamed. I screamed.
I made my parents do it. My mother's allergic,
so what, it's their fault, they raised us."

I'm six. 1974. Somebody's New York apartment,
white rug, many people. They say "schmatte." They say
"schmooze," they say "schwarze." They wear
bead necklaces, interesting belts, plastic white
sunglasses propped on their heads. Nixon's
resigning on black-and-white TV. He says
nobody gave him anything except a dog.
I climb on Sophie's lap. She smells like olives.
She's drinking a martini. "And," I say to Leah,
2004, "I said something. What did I say?"

"You said 'poor Nixon,'" Leah says. "'Nobody
gave him anything but a little puppy dog—
didn't he have a mommy and poppy?' Nixon's dog speech
was before you were born. You're remembering
a rerun. You were on my lap, not Sophie's. Sophie
was flirting with Arthur."

1980, Leah and Sophie voted for Reagan.
My father wouldn't speak to them for six months.

Now he tells me the good side
of Ariel Sharon. I don't speak to him much.
Leah says: "Arthur was her first Republican.
After Sophie married him, she was happy
for awhile." Leah lights a cigarette off her
burnt-down cigarette—curlicues
of smoke. She says: "I just can't understand how
your father became a Conservative Jew."

I say "I haven't spoken to my sister
for four years. I am unreasonable—
sometimes. I have a hot temper—
sometimes. But I am not envious, I am not
entirely uncharitable,
at all times I try to behave as if I realize
the world does not revolve around
my feelings. Above all, I am
not deranged, I do not take out
my problems on other people's *cats*."

Leah says, "Sophie thought you were like her.
Do you think you're like her?" She puts
her cigarette in the ashtray, I pick it up,
take my first drag in ten years. It burns. Aches.
Sour, it stings. "People still buy his
paintings," Leah says. "For historical
value, I guess. I don't know what he was to her."

Leah twists her head. "Just take it now," she says.
I take down the painting. Leah wipes her eyes.
"I don't know why I'm crying.
If she came in this room now I'd leave.
If she opened her mouth, I'd slap it."

The Hawk

*On July 21, 2005, Rep. Allyson Y. Schwartz (D., Pa.) voted for a bill
to extend the Patriot Act for another 10 years. President Bush hailed the vote.*

From the playground's biggest tree's biggest branch
the hawk through daylight drops to the monkeybars
top deck, claws sunk in its plunder. The hawk
shakes its gray-brown feathers, leans, with its beak
unzips the little squirrel suit, probes into the hot mess.
Nothing bothers it. The raincoated tourist grabs
his wife's wrist knobs, gabbles a strange language,
transfixed by the bird, and the scaly foot closes down.
A mom clamps her hand over the eyes of her kid,
his face so small her hand covers it. She hustles him
bellowing away; he wrenches at her fingers,
will break them, *will*, if he can, to see. Watchers
gasp, groan, video. "I love this," a man whispers,
hands in his suit pockets. "I'm a hunter but I never
get to hunt anymore, so I love this!" The hawk
from the carcass extracts a bit of bloody intestine.
Flips it long, thin, looplike, over his beak. A gewgaw.
Tilts, eats. Gets another. Loops and eats again.

Running while Screaming

Here come two girls running at me hard
and plump, thudding, almost falling, flailing
arms, 12, maybe 13, coughing laughter,
spitting with it, splitting up to
dodge around me and an old guy
with his old dog, mom with stroller;
rejoin, reach with their hands like passing
the baton, like stretching for the gold ring,
keep running while screaming—

Me and Ti-Anne dawdle home from seventh grade.
The street long, downed leaves whisking
on sidewalks, lawns. Ahead, a mailman
in uniform shorts it's getting too cold for,
his legs all hairy. Ti-Anne does or I start;
I join or she does, *nice legs, ooh baby,*
got mail for me? Ti-Anne tips her head back
to open her throat, lets out such a scream
like a whistle a boy makes with two fingers
in his mouth. *Whit-wheeeewwww!* I can't do it
so hey *Legs!* I yell *I love your hairy legs!*
The mailman keeps digging in his sack,
walking up and down porch steps that sag,
snapping rubber bands off mail stacks,
slides envelopes in slots, *Oooh Mr. Legs,*
doesn't he hear us? now we're caught up—
Ti-Anne grabs my arm, hissy snickers
hh hh hh trying to hold in our laughter
almost feels like being sick, our eyes watering,
faces hot with it—the mailman turns,
squints, smiles wide: "Thanks for the whistles
and comments, ladies!" He raises his brows,
makes a face full of wrinkles, he winks—

Ti-Anne shrieks or I do—we take off
screaming at a joke I don't get but it
scares me we know if we don't stop
we'll fall down will die of it but
can't stop running while screaming.

The Drunkard's Bar

The drunkard's bar on Canal Saint Martin
has scrabbled windows, ancient posters,
is shoebox shaped. Tranquil bartender,
his unperturbable wife, boisterous
unlonesome drunkards squeezed at the bar
dropped in this Xmas morning out of the old
Paris that hardly is anymore. Drunks cheery
in morose drunkard style, slow of tongue,
forgetting whole paragraphs of their lives.
There's a slight danger it could all slide
bone-tired to angry. But, nah, not today,
bumping around under the *biere de noel* sign,
cogitating into their wine, cheapest of schemes
for morning hangover headache relief. *Je mens*,

I'm *lying*, the lady drunk claims in giggles.
She lies from habit not malice about everything
and everybody. Oldtimey accordion music
on the back-wall jukebox, its sliding lights,
heatless not-hearth blinking against sapped
north latitude winter window sun. The man
in dirty suede feeds the box his several francs,
dances his belly up/down the room, sings,
of course, "La Vie en Rose," along with Piaf.
The lady, in her plushy coat, speckled
like dog fur, collar up (it's chilly in here),
with wilted lips, watches, swivels back,
then front, then back to the bar. She sings along,
her different song, *je mens*. Laugh and forced laugh

hunker up in her eyes. Her voice asunder,
hoarse. Tinsel paper angels glint above where
aqua smoke rises, hangs, among high glasses.

She spins her stool. She sings. I don't know
the words. I know what they mean: *I dangle,*
I dangle my very old shoes, I sit alone,
he lurches past, he likes me I think, she sings,
or maybe not, but you know in the fairy tale
the girl who was so good she spat jewels
when she talked, and the other who wasn't
and so spat toads, snakes, salamanders?
It's not true. There was only one girl and
what came out of her mouth was an iguana,
and its lewd toes were spangled with emeralds.

Go to Your Room

In her observatory, her little red room,
the daughter sings "Do Ya Think I'm Sexy"
into her hairbrush. It's not true
what they're thinking about her. She's lying
across her bed, laughing at her mother
clanking something downstairs
to let everyone know who's angry
and right. *Turn down the music!* The daughter
fills her mouth with 17 Big Red sticks
from a 24-pack, eats pretzels too, mixing in
salt and crumbs. *Turn down the music!*
Sunlight gaps into the room.

The daughter belly down, stomach
muscles tight, head hanging
off the bed-edge, arms straight out
before her. *Turn down the music!*
Eight blue glass marbles between
her prehensile toes, one
marble between each two. She
claps her foot soles, clicking
the marbles, little worlds,
together. She turns down
the music, writes "lassitude" in
the dust on the radio.

The daughter eats icing with her
finger from a bowl on her lap:
Powdered sugar, margarine, vanilla.
She made it herself from a
recipe on the box. There are escapes and
they are true things.

Mother, that ass, doesn't know.
                                                    Sun
blasts the curtains open like legs.

Empty Woman

Amigos de las Mujeres de Juarez march, Valentine's Day, 2004

Store mannequins in Juarez wear
staring eyes, enamel, bold. Ni una mas
marchers for the dead girls chant. In
every bride-gown skirt displayed
in windows down the dusty street,
pastel flowers nest like
gift-wrapped rodents. February,
but the sun's hot. I have to pee. Skimpy
Rio Grande trickles in its concrete trough
behind us; squat sterile El Paso towers
and a bridge. Ahead the NAFTA
Center, its gift of same wages/higher-
cost-of-living. Sugar skulls. Drugstore
signboards pitch cheap
no-prescription Viagra. Dead
girls we chant for. Ni una mas.
    . . .

Ni una mas. I buy a Coke at a bar
to use the bathroom. My feet stick to
the floor leaving. Here comes the arty
protest dress, giantsize, symbolizing
missing women, crucified above
our heads on poles, jouncing, swaying,
made of wood and wire, hair and
caution tape, plastic doll eyes crying
plastic glued-on tears. A college kid
passes me a pole to hold. My arms shake
with the weight. I need to join a gym.
The skirt blows across my face.
Where are my friends?
I don't know anybody here.

The dress transparent, sunlight
pours through thin cotton—
the dress kicking, fighting backward
at its spars. A boy and a girl come up
to help: "we saw you struggling."
I hand them my pole, shake out
my arms: a tiny effort that aches. I can
see through to the red construction
paper heart pinned over
where her ribs and where a mole
you could kiss would be.

At Advent, the Waiting Room

We small army say if you turn time
backwards, Mary goes back to Bethlehem,
the lowing of the cattle, the comfort of straw.
Labor's just as terrible, if not worse, in reverse,
but then the swelling hurt subsides; her breasts
grow lighter, de-manufacturing the milk
that would have fed the god. Mary still
remembers the strange unraveling. Therefore
no one ever bears, no one ever
bears the whole world's weight alone again.

Sugar

I'm trying to quit, licking chocolate
off my fingers. I'm the new counterperson
at Miss Julie's Sweet Shoppe. I nibble
scones, snack on truffles. Sugar sweat,
sugar grit jumps me almost out of my skin.
It itches. *Eat what you want,* Miss Julie says.
But don't lick your fingers. My head buzzes;
harp music; I feel slightly sick. Sun blasts
pure light across the big plate glass windows.
I'm gaining weight. Miss Julie says *Don't worry,
you'll quit. Soon all you'll want to eat is bitter greens.
That's what sugar does to you.* She tucks
her shimmery flower-pattern shirt
into her blue jeans. *Just call me Julie!*
Miss Julie says. She's one of us—
young for a boss. She says *Turn the carrot cupcakes,*
Every orange-icing carrot
must point at the customer. *Fold the linen.*
I lay it clean in wicker baskets.
Steam the milk. The espresso machine spigot
screams, subsides in hisses. Rain splatters
the door. *Make new price signs.*
I use the pink or purple markers.
I'm allowed to draw in one or two flowers.

A nitpicky, dreamy, easy job—horrible
and pleasant. I sweep, bored as I want to be.
Don't touch the chocolate! Don't lick your fingers!
I lick my fingers. Pink girly dining room
music box desire. The exhaust fan
sends sugar stench out to the pavement.
I Windex handprint fog
customers leave on the display case

like they want to dive in! Miss Julie says.
I rest in protocol's encompassing allure.
A strand of my hair catches on angelfood cake.
She hands me a hairnet. "Thanks," I say,
little sister being fitted into big sister's world.
Next week you'll learn how to decorate cupcakes!
She pays me $5 an hour.

                             I find a new job for $8.
Miss Julie takes me to her basement office,
sits at her desk—a door set on milk crates—
writes my last check. *I'm disappointed in you,*
she says. "Miss Julie—" I say. *Just Julie!*
she snaps, cutting me off. Smudges
under her eyes like bruises, like she's sad,
insomniac. I want to explain—
I like this job, the tasks, the customers,
the sticky sugar gack—I love being disgusted.
We took the trouble to train you, she says.
You're being disloyal. You showed real promise.
She hands me my check and—she's one of
the good bosses—adds a cash bonus. She says
I feel like you're saying to me "fuck you Julie."

I want to explain—$3 more,
times 40 hours, it's $120 extra a week—
but it would sound so disloyal.
Sweet smells of muffin fill my sinuses,
stop my mouth. I hand her the hairnet.
I say "Fuck you, sugar."

First Boyfriend, 14

New Adam's apple
destroying his soprano,
he bleats, tucks his chin
down to his neck. Mothballs
in his throat, can't
figure out where to
put his voice. Harmony
hiccups away. After
choir practice he runs
barefoot, jeans rolled up,
through deep snow on a dare,
naked also to the waist,
mooing like the minotaur.

Some Loud Men, Some Women

cutting their eyes sideways, inhaling air
smoky and clean, the light dim and constant
no excuse for this feeling

of intoxication—but tiny branches
press up against the window, no leaves
but are they gold, are they green, what the sun
does to them, the shadow,
                                        and you, love

I don't mean to make this personal, but
I am sure of that. You and city and life
and home and history and shopping
like a bunch of cars
getting backed up on a turnpike
one of those massive fog pileups
cars spanking off one another's bumpers

they make you laugh
till you're coughing with it, eyes leaking

insurance policies everywhere jump
a couple hundred bucks and a motorcycle zips
or unzips our sense of elsewhere
crawling across the screen of our brains
and the neighborhood children clutch
their Jennifer-the-Friendly-Faun dolls

as they scamper across jungle gym bridges
boys hang hard onto joysticks so do girls

children may be distractible, we may be distractible

a whale caught in the Delaware River
his tail damaged and they are trying to swim him
back down to where the salt is thicker
water deeper, less polluted with leads, chlordanes, PCBs
and he can turn somersaults and find a whale lover
as the sun breaks like an egg over Liberty Tower

sometimes it's nice the way you're good—
I probably—was I?— sure of that . . .

Pablo Picasso Was Never Called an Asshole

Well some people try to pick up girls
and get called assholes.
This never happened to Pablo Picasso.
    Jonathan Richman and The Modern Lovers

I was in the park with everybody, where everybody drives up
with six-packs of Bud to watch the sun fall.
The hour the sun's colors began to mix in the river
I knew I'd be late, I took off running. I'm running fast
as I can to hear him sing,
past cars, cars going, cars turning
off and parked and dark
inside, Clubs like erections
locked down over their steering columns,
SUVs rocking their box bodies
like pea-brained stegosauruses
taking potholes, taking corners slow.
A low-slung city, cicadas pounding in the trees. *Slow down,*
some bum calls from his boredom doorway.
My feet in sneaks killing. Something always aching,
killing or itching. Something laying
marks on my skin. Or no marks, baby irritations.
Am I sending the wrong message? I have no messages.
By contrast everyone else has messages they thought up themselves.
To be on time for his show would mean
none of it mattered. His small face screamed fuck yous
going backwards out the door. That gave me
something to hate besides myself. OK, I ran away first,
now I run towards him. Is that pat or what?
    . . .

After the month's best orgasm,
we're at the orchestra, it's glowing like I'm glowing.
I'm in this mode: nothing else

but me. I become
aware of the music: *Petrouchka*. A dance more often
played than performed. Outside coming here
no moon no stars no stars no moon,
just pale gray of night clouds against
dark blacky gray and wind
bending down the small
trees. Now that woman's hat blocks the view:
I lean into him to see double basses,
tubas. I like her fake flowers,
half crumpled and perky, smelling
of rain, pinned by a pearl hatpin
out of Edith Wharton. We clap. We leave.
Notice how he could be any man, no specific one.
   . . .
On the way home, the sound of wipers
a black sound. A wet couple
out there half in, half out of a doorway, drunk, climbing
into each others' mouths, his fists against
her back. The rain contains
pinches of light; tree twigs resolve
to circles with the lights behind them,
light makes me dizzy; I'm tired
of hearing myself complain but driving
away from him could it just once not be raining?

Chicken Factory

song

Look: white feathers, blowing on roadways
Won't you come back sir, won't you come back sir?

A lady sleeps badly after you go
Pillows a-tangle. Whirlpools her sheets
Won't you come back sir, come back soon?

They pluck chickens, they pluck hens
Out of work men doing tricks with matches
Strike on the jeans seam, strike on the boot heel
Oh now sir why won't you come back home?

Flames from their bodies lighting their cigarettes
Tiny fires toss, spit in the night wind

Look at all the dead feathers blowing
Come home and see your darling

III.

My Brother Is Getting Arrested Again

My brother is getting arrested again.

What does he want? What does he know?
We can't talk politics. He doesn't have politics.
I'm helpless with him.

My brother is getting arrested again.

He is not weeding community gardens.
He is not climbing on roofs to bang
with hammer on shingles, admire
his arm-hairs going gold in the sun.

My brother is getting arrested again.

My mother makes sarcastic remarks
and bails him out.
They can't talk politics.
She's helpless with him.

He pushes hard at a sawhorse barricade,
black bandana up over his nose.
He shouts *this is what democracy looks like.*

My brother is getting arrested again.

He's not lending a hand at needle exchanges.
Not fishing from pier's end with his best buddy, Dad.
He might be facing the incoming clouds.

He's not wearing pinstripes, seersucker, wingtips,
not dressing down for casual Friday. He doesn't care
about the future of Krispy Kreme stock.

My father clears his throat. He says "being pro-Palestinian
is anti-Semitic." They can't talk politics.
My father is helpless with him.

The barricade breaks,
the yellow do-not-cross crossbeam
smacks to the ground.

My little sister says, snippily, "I agree with him—
in principle." They don't talk politics.
She's helpless with him.

My brother is getting arrested again.

A sudden melee, my brother disappearing.
He sucks in others like a star imploding.

He's down, he's lifted away,
wrists latched behind his back.

Now he stinks from the heat on the prison bus.
Now he's stuffed in a holding cell with eight other protesters.
Now they take apart the sandwiches they get in jail.
They eat the bread—they toss
the orange limp cheese square at the wall.
It sticks. Collaborative chem-processed
chance-operation artwork. It's a whale!
It's the mayor! It's the moon!
No sleep for three days and three nights,
the lights never go out, the delirious
buzzed noise of themselves. They can't
take a shower. They sass the guards,
chant protest chants. *This is what democracy
smells* like. The funniest joke they ever told.

My brother signs his name on a paper, gets out.

And now?

Is he hopping dancelessly obedient
to directional arrows on a suburban mall machine
called Dance Dance Revolution?

Is he driving a waverunner in circles and laughing
on the filthy Delaware, our city's river?
Is he advanced degreeing in the even-weathered West?

Is he climbing Mt. Rainier?

Nope. Come rain, or shine, or sweat, or hope,
my brother is getting arrested again.

Used One Speed, Princeton

I painted my bike purple,
it's finding a brown to fade to.
Along the long slow curve of streets
gelato-colored houses change in dusk
to colors of dove. On my one speed, life is plain.
Here the mudflats are called a river. I am feeling
new muscles in my thighs. My fat fenders
guard me from mud-splat. Look at these tires:
wide as trenches. My second-grade teacher said
"sit up straight." My ex-fiancé used to
put his hand through his hair,
make a fist, say "that's just them
trying to keep the working class docile."
The houses dim, colors of soap, the shaped kind
you put in little dishes, that shrink and melt
to goo. I sometimes feel rather shaky
but that's OK. I guard against regret,
disapproval, those middle-aged emotions.
I am still young, I feel I am. If I wanted I could
ride no-hands, my bike so steady, arms out
like that guy in Goya's *Third of May, 1808,*
with the white shirt, his eyes wide open,
facing death. I don't.   I squint my eyes
against gnats. And so, and so, I was saying,
when a certain feeling comes over me,
something that feels like foolish bravery,
I glide, concede, I sit straight up.

Stealing from Lehigh Dairy

Her black socks and her white ones
are littered together over the sofa,
soft strewn piano keys. Her shirt
arms and pant legs wrestle up
over the table, into the unworking
fireplace. Deflated bodies hug and
twine and twine and twine and hug.

Something needs to be done:
her boyfriend took the milkcrates
in the breakup. Thirteen weeks
since he went. Color-coded, the crates
held everything: their lives. Red,
his T-shirts; orange, hers. Camisoles,
underpants, bandanas, bras, books,
CDs, compilation tapes they made
together—*Dance Groove 3, '97*
on the little sticker—each had its
crate. Only their dirty laundry
mingled in the Lehigh Dairy gray one—
the crate he left her. She slept
in his bed for months before she knew
crates were there too, under the board
under the foam pad, under her and him
twining their arms and legs together,
each with its warning: use by other
than registered owner punishable by law.

He left the foam pad—filthy on the floor.
Thirteen weeks: nothing's sorted. One day
she put the compact discs into shoeboxes
that used to hold her party shoes,
but next morning woke to find her silvery

sandals, her see-through pumps jumbled,
as if they snuck and crept at night like her,
hooking heels in sneak mouths.

Something needs to be done. She drives
to the supermarket back alley loading dock,
night near dawn, but dark still, and full
of stars and trees, feeble stars, she means,
and city trees, hugging the darkness
out of the darkness into their small still
selves. The alley's unlit, streetlights failed
or cracked by some kid's rock. The Lehigh
crates are stacked on the platform, faded
out of their gray blue gray orange by night
to dark and light. She climbs up, throws
crates down, eight, sixteen, twenty, more.
She throws and listens to their *bank*
and *bonk*, their *clack-clank*. The noise
brings a bike cop, he brakes up, fast—
yo, hold up there!

She stands on the dock,
four final crates, two
per hand, on the dock lip
painted yellow for warning.
I'm just getting crates,
she says, her most
middle-middle class
accent. The cop says
you're stealing. She says
I have to, it's my life.
A pause. *Well make
less noise then,*
the cop says, rides on.

She'll jump down now, load them
in her car, till the car's a cage full
of smaller cages. Before she jumps,
she knows she'll fall the six feet
(a boyfriend's height) to the vicious
cement. She'll scrape her palms,
she'll twist an ankle, her ankle
will swell, her palms will sting,
grit in the gashes. She'll stack
the crates in her living room,
leave them three weeks, a month,
longer, in four- or five-story stacks.

She'll shift them sometimes
but leave them empty. Sometimes
sun will come through the
eastern windows, seem to clean
the mess, bring the empty crates
odd tints, play them like colored
keys. She looks down at her
feet on the yellow dock danger
stripe. She knows sun will seem
to dirty the place the more.
She knows, predicts. Through
night denseness
                    she jumps.

Three Times Only

Twice at the movies. The first time, the colliery band,
after a terrible time of layoffs and disloyalties,
crowds into the upper double-decker bus deck.
As the bus swings past parliament's night-spires
they take out their meticulously-polished brasses,
some silver-colored, some gold,
and strike up "The Internationale." It was the music made him.

The second time because the heroine
in another final scene sobs so convincingly
at getting what she wants. It was a perfect sob.

The third time at his brother's funeral,
at the funny stories his brother's best friend told.
Small reddenings about my husband's face.
In the pit of his palm,
a crumpled tissue like a carnation.

The Conference Notes

"Don't interview me," I say when Lynnie and Mel
ask about boyfriends. "I have one I'm mean to.
He's in my bed now with his boots on."

Mel says, "My husband hates me."

Lynnie says, "I just like men.
Do you think I ought not to? Think I ought
to be more picky?" She likes their company, likes everything
about them, their tempers and humors, their thinking,
their physical necessities, and destinies, "of course their bodies
too. That's how I like men. Some don't, I do, OK."

Mel says, "She's writing down everything you say."

Lynnie deals with men "the way a horsewoman
deals with horses": contracts into the long slow process
of letting the other creature tell her how to get it
to do what she wants. "With men," she says,
"that can be speeded up." Is she right?

Maybe she just wants a place
where she can turn in and in and in on herself
like some garrulous extroverted blabby kid
who weirdly goes silent for long periods of time.

Lynnie takes out a pack of Merits,
puts pretzel sticks one by one
into the corners of her mouth between
her back teeth, shuts her mouth on them,

brushes invisible salt off her lap.
"These taste horrible with cigarette smoke."

HOSPITALITY LOUNGE. A PERFECT MIRROR

I scribble notes. Democratic Women's
Conference, 1996. Women walk
long hypnotized parabolas across the lounge,
primp at windows on a street so dark
they make perfect mirrors. Check teeth,
grimace lipstick, neaten hair, wring waists
to find their slimmest angles. Mel:
"Must look funny from the other side."

LET'S ALL DIE

"Give me one," Mel says. They
play hooky from speeches,
panel presentations.

"Sure," Lynnie says. "We've had
a few drinks." She lights Mel's cigarette,
raises her own as if in a toast.
"Let's all die."

They take little sips,
hardly inhaling. They're not
much older than me.

QUICK SHADOWS

Quick shadows witch the mirror window:
surge behind the glass, run and heave,
make our bodies into protesters. Almost
we can hear them. Crash-voiced,
bellowing, no words come through.

Mel pulls her nametag, stuck with threads
and yarn, off her turtleneck sweater.
TV crews outside the lounge blast light.
This changed everything. Or maybe not.
Placards, open shouting mouths, arms
like boughs of trees in a storm, as if
sheet lightning filled a sky, stayed lit.
Signs bob-bob stapled to wood spars,
bed-sheets strung between poles, holes
cut so they don't strain in rising wind.
Lights turn people teak, ruddy. Bullhorn
shouting sounds like *no light! no light!*
(I must have heard wrong.) Kids link arms,
lie down in the street. I'm unable
to move, watching, in my leatherette armchair.
I write: *chair creaks.* Thunder: more cops.
It's on the lounge TV. People run
behind the newscaster, her hair lifts
all of a piece, falls the same way. A cop
bumps a girl on a bike with his motorcycle tire,
she falls, it happens fast but seems slow motion,
commentating TV natter always with us,
we see it here, we see it out there, the Coke
machine hisses, the girl's braids fly out,
panties flash. I write: *color of a handcuffed sky.*
She catches herself, blows on her sore hands.
She's not much younger than me.
A cop puts plastic cuffs on her, pulls them tight.
"Poor thing," says Lynnie. And Mel:
"Why would you wear a skirt for that?"

CLEANING HOUSE

Years later, cleaning house before
a move, I find the conference notes. They're
hard to read. Scattered words. One sentence:
What if this were life affirming?

Did I mean that?

My boyfriend left long ago: I harangued him away.
I married. (I just like men.) I never wrote the article,
never saw the women again. It's not such a big deal
what happened between now and then. I went
out to the protesters. It's the end of a beginning. I go
home and kick the sole
of my boyfriend's boot: it stuck out
from the futon on the floor.

OUTSIDE

I stand far back, scared
in the sunken street, sniff my scarf,
filmy green with butterflies. Cops in pairs
carry off the girl with the other kids—
her body slack—her bike
abandoned by the curb.

I come back in. Mel says,
"You think they're right?"
Lynnie says, "Whatever they want
that bad, I hope they get it."
Mel: "That would teach them."
Lynnie: "What's it for again?"

I stood at the window, retied my scarf,
tried to look at, not through it, tried to make an elegant knot.
But can't see myself. There's too much light.

Slack Morning, Reading Sterne for the First Time at 36,
after My Husband Has Mocked Me for Years for My Omission,
Princeton, Early Fall

"I'm 15," he says, "determined to be an atheist, determined
to be socialist, to drag myself out of the Victorian swamp
that was Northeast Philly back then. I walk into Leary's,
pick up this old used book Tristram Shandy I never heard of,
open it and see the marble page, which really was
color-plate marble—"
                              His sinus problem overrides his story,
he dangles his arms, goes half-upside down to clear his head.

Another beheading on NPR, a musical interlude and then
the rat terrier commentator asserts "resolve," insists "will,"

but the rightwing thinktanker who's actually been thinking a little
      admits
"once a whole population of a country doesn't want you,
you have to go . . ."

                              The one dove I see outside the apartment window
becomes two,
then nine or ten—
wittering among the yellow leafing flashbulb of a tulip tree.

Envy

Saliva comes up in the mouth. The fish cook
twists the dial to high. The range hisses out
its invisible gas. He lights a match
walking away, tosses it back at the burner.
Gas foomps up into a fire corona, continually
licks itself into its own self-perpetuating life.
"One time I missed," the fish cook says.
Ti-Anne and I eat lunch here often; he tells us stories.
"The match fell. I lit another, threw it behind me.
The air went up in blue flames.
My skin wasn't burned but my eyebrows,
eyelashes, arm-hairs, nose-hairs: all gone!"
He grins. "You see I didn't learn my lesson!"

The fish cook has wrinkles laid over his baby face,
or baby-face shoved in underneath his wrinkles.
He pours wine, fish stock, into a skillet. Juice
sizzles, jumps off oil onto his apron. Violent heat.
"Here you go girls," he says, slides us our plates.
"I'm eleven weeks pregnant," Ti-Anne says. "I only
told my in-laws yesterday!" She throws her arms
around me. I hear her hands thwack my back;
her jaw jabs my ear. Outside the window
a red Escalade drives by in shiny winter light.
"Congratulations!" the fish cook says.

I meet Ti-Anne for gossip, relief, remembrance,
measuring our careers—"like guys do their dicks,"
Ti-Anne likes to say—playing hooky from work.
Who's doing what. Who we used to sleep with when.
We talk so much we don't know what we say.
"I Know What Boys Like" comes on the sound system.

I used to play it on my college radio show when
I liked thinking songs were what I was. Ti-Anne
has braids, many troubles, dainty manners;
today she chatters, munches, slurps, discards
shellfish hardware. We fork up crab scraps,
mussels, garlic cloves, out of the bouillabaisse.
Ti-Anne, you're leaving me behind.

I spoon broth in. Gulping, leaning forward,
like you have to at a counter. She's telling me
how happy she is: "No more Paris now
ever again. No Mantua, Madrid. No more
late-night band gigs. I'll have to drive
the turnpike speed limit! We can't afford it,
it's moronic. My insurance sucks.
My marriage is shaky enough . . ."

"Jim and I are trying too. Half," I say,
half-lying. Not to say *do I have to do your stupid*
baby shower just because you did my wedding one
I say "All marriages are shaky—
nothing else would keep us interested.
Remember we had the same repeating dream?
The boyfriend dies, we stand, in our respective
sleeps, delivering elegies or silent looks. Real tears
wet our faces. Everyone loves us. We wake up
sad. We always said we'd only marry when
our boyfriends stopped dying in our dreams."

Ti-Anne puts her elbows on the counter. "In fact,
in dreams, in mine, I mean, my husband still dies,"
she says. *Ti-Anne, you stink.* She says: "Now I'll
never be a superstar." In regret or relief,
I can't tell which, won't ask. "Congrats, really,"

the fish cook says. He lights a match walking away,
tosses it back at the burner. I hear the thump of fire.
Ti-Anne laughs, flashes her hands like fingerflames.
"*Foomp!*" she says. "It's like you're leaving me behind."

In a Station of the Metro

Here I am in a blue shirt, suffering heat,
feeling hateful. An express train
slows on the far track through
its jail of pillars; flashes
snaps of its riders like pictographs
hanging onto overhead bars; sighs
out of sight. Overtired, late home,
holding bags, turning 37, I remember
being ten: the train filled with bright light
doesn't stop, moves on away;
knowing, with a kind of pleasure
in what I didn't know then was
inexorability's ease, I could never get on.

Death, a poem in two parts

1.

Late afternoon, snow starts. I'm walking
with my husband, as we do, in the city,
talking, as often we also do, about the problem of
putting dead animals in poems.
                              "Too obvious,
invisible, symbolic," I say. My husband agrees,
or might not be listening. "Maybe," he says.
"It disappears into its facts." Snowflakes like fingertip
touches on our faces. We turn the corner,
Ninth St. Market—kale, collards, garlic piles—
bootleg videos, clap-to-start singing Xmas elf dolls—
and "look!"—my husband pokes me, points—
a dead deer is pushed into this poem. Junior
the butcher rolls it forward, laid out across
a low dolly: a button buck, tiny spikes,
red eyes clouded over—stiff like a toy horse
knocked on its side. Hunters freeze their kill,
bring it to Junior to make into "roasts, chops—
hamburger, mostly," Junior says. "Ow!"
He dances awkward around the hooves. "Dead
but still kicking—I knew it wouldn't fit in the door.
I tell them 'Cut the legs at the knee, you're not
losing meat.' They can't find the joint." He bends;
his five-inch fibrox-handle straight-edge knife
slides in the knee-knuckle. The leg end falls.
By now you're imagining a stereotypical butcher—
big man, tall, gore-stained apron, toupee—
and you're almost right. Junior's never
marked with blood; he raises orchids
which curl their panicles and lippy scapes
above his fancy sausages. He paints Renoir

copies he shows among carcasses in his window:
plushy naked ladies look ethereal
beside real meat. Second hoof, third hoof.
Frozen blood on frozen belly hair. Closest
I've been to a dead animal with its skin on.
Gauze over the city, gauze really is what the
sky looks like, clouded over. Snow detaches
down to our world in dit-dots. Fourth hoof.
Junior's hand follows where the knife feels to go.

2.

"Ow," I say, when we get home. "Don't touch
my body, your hands are too cold. But
I'll hold them in my armpits till they're warm."
Curtains printed with small red flowers
hiked back. Night. Asterisks of snow. His hands
warmer now. Snow in swirls across the window,
invisible, symbolic, obvious.

ACKNOWLEDGMENTS

Grateful thanks to the Humanities Council at Princeton University, the Leeway Foundation, and the Pew Fellowships in the Arts, which provided support during the writing of these poems.

Poems from this manuscript have been published in: *American Poetry Review*: "At Advent, the Waiting Room"; *Antioch Review*: "Neat Hair"; *5 A.M.*: "American Brass"; *Indiana Review*: "Chicken Factory"; *Kenyon Review*: "Gal Noir," "Used One Speed, Princeton"; *Ontario Review*: "First Boyfriend, 14," "Go to Your Room," "In a Station of the Metro," "Slack Morning, Reading Sterne for the First Time at 36, after My Husband Has Mocked Me for Years for My Omission, Princeton, Early Fall," "Sugar"; *Ploughshares*: "Shooting Kinesha"; *Poetry*: "Aunt Leah, Aunt Sophie and the Negro Painter," "Running while Screaming"; *Prairie Schooner*: "The Falling"; *Puerto del Sol*: "Empty Woman"; *Threepenny Review*: "Broken Radios," "The Conference Notes," "Death, a poem in two parts," "Doll Ritual," "My Brother Is Getting Arrested Again"; *TriQuarterly*: "Cordless," "The Drunkard's Bar," "Jubilate South Philly, City 14," "Stealing from Lehigh Dairy"; *Yale Review*: "Three Times Only."

"Best of Show" was published as a broadside by Pressed Wafer, Boston, MA (2004).

"The Hawk" was published under the title "Guts" in different versions in *Ars Botanica*, a handmade art-book by Enid Mark/ELM Press (2004) and in the anthology *Birds in the Hand* (2004) and appeared, in its present form, at the Web site www.personnagesobscurs.com.

The first section of "Pablo Picasso Was Never Called an Asshole" was published under the title "Running to Hear Him Sing" in *Prairie Schooner*.

"Chicken Factory," "Death, a poem in two parts," and "My Brother is Getting Arrested Again" were republished by *Poetry Daily* (www.poems .com).

"Shooting Kinesha" was awarded a Pushcart Prize and republished in *Pushcart Prize XXX: Best of the Small Presses* (2005), and received the 2005 Cohen Award from *Ploughshares*.

The lines quoted as an epigraph to the poem "Pablo Picasso Was Never Called an Asshole" were written by Jonathan Richman, published by Modern Love Songs; administration by Joel S. Turtle.